Man

The Royal
Photographic
Society _____

RPS

A
book of
postcards

Pomegranate Artbooks / San Francisco

Pomegranate Artbooks
Box 6099
Rohnert Park, CA 94927

ISBN 1-56640-238-7
Pomegranate Catalog No. A656

Pomegranate publishes books of postcards on a wide range of subjects.
Please write to the publisher for more information

© 1993 The Royal Photographic Society

Designed by Allen Boyce Eddington
Printed in Korea

From its very beginnings, photography has been used for portraiture. The desire to record the human face and form has been an energizing force of all art forms, and photography is no different.

The Royal Photographic Society Collection contains examples of every aspect of the portrait, from the carte de visite (the most popular form of photography in the nineteenth century, which enabled everyone to have access to the likenesses of the famous and the infamous of the day), to the hologram.

Photographers practising outside the commercial studio, many represented in this selection, reworked the standard portrait format to emphasize qualities other than the purely visual in the sitter.

In the early 1900s the artist-photographer Alvin Langdon Coburn revolutionized the portrait format in his books *Men of Mark* and *More Men of Mark*, roll calls of the artistically famous. His photographs of artists, writers and musicians are visual representations of genius. These men are different. Like Julia Margaret Cameron before him, Coburn took portraits of ideas. He was interested in spiritual rather than physical beauty. He could easily have taken Cameron's portrait of John Herschel. Coburn's Rodin could be by her.

Portraits by Fred Holland Day show a meshing of these two qualities. In general, Day's men are anonymous, yet they have great physical beauty and a strong spiritual core, as epitomised in the portrait of Kahlil Gibran. Steichen's portraits show more concern with the confidence of his subjects and the power they emanate, qualities that were reflective of his own nature.

Overall, these portraits tell us as much about the photographer as the sitter. In many cases, the photographer is as much a respected expert in his or her field as is the subject. An image observed in this context imparts a feeling of mutual respect between photographer and sitter, thereby strengthening the image's aesthetic and historic merits.

Many of these photographs were donated to the Royal Photographic Society by the photographers themselves. They not only represent the epitome of their work but also provide an enduring record of man and his capabilities.

——Pam Roberts, curator, The Royal Photographic Society, Bath, England

Images of Man

Man with Book (Kahlil Gibran)
By Fred Holland Day (American, 1864–1933)
Platinum print, c. 1897

Pomegranate, Box 6099, Rohnert Park, CA 94927

© The Royal Photographic Society

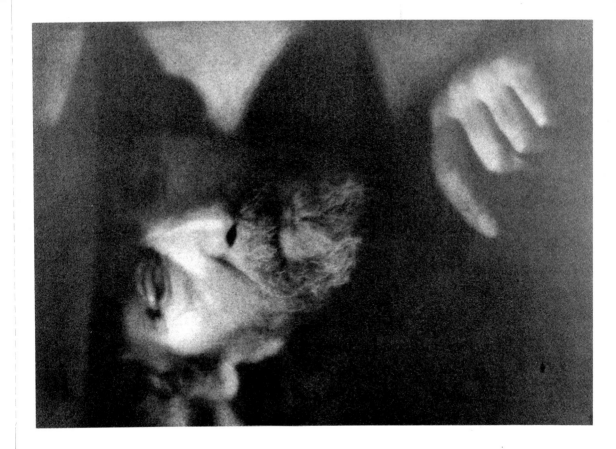

Images of Man

Mannerkopf
By Professor Rudolf Koppitz (Austrian, 1884–1936)
Bromoil Transfer, 1928

Pomegranate, Box 6099, Rohnert Park, CA 94927

© The Royal Photographic Society

Images of Man

Man's Head (The Italian)
By Fred Holland Day (American, 1864–1933)
Platinum print, c. 1906

Pomegranate, Box 6099, Rohnert Park, CA 94927

© The Royal Photographic Society

Images of Man

The Astronomer, Sir John Herschel
By Julia Margaret Cameron (English, 1815–1879)
Albumen print, 1867

Pomegranate, Box 6099, Rohnert Park, CA 94927

© The Royal Photographic Society

Images of Man

Sir Richard Burton
By Julia Margaret Cameron (English, 1815–1879)
Albumen print, c. 1870

Pomegranate, Box 6099, Rohnert Park, CA 94927

© The Royal Photographic Society

Images of Man

Aldous Huxley
By Pirie MacDonald (American, 1867–1942)
From *Photograms of the Year*, 1925–1926
Halftone print

Pomegranate, Box 6099, Rohnert Park, CA 94927

© The Royal Photographic Society

Images of Man

George Bernard Shaw
By Alvin Langdon Coburn
(English, b. U.S., 1882–1966)
Photogravure from *Camerawork*, January 1908

Pomegranate, Box 6099, Rohnert Park, CA 94927

© The Royal Photographic Society

Images of Man

Cyril Scott
By Alvin Langdon Coburn
(English, b. U.S., 1882–1966)
Bromide print, 1915

Pomegranate, Box 6099, Rohnert Park, CA 94927

© The Royal Photographic Society

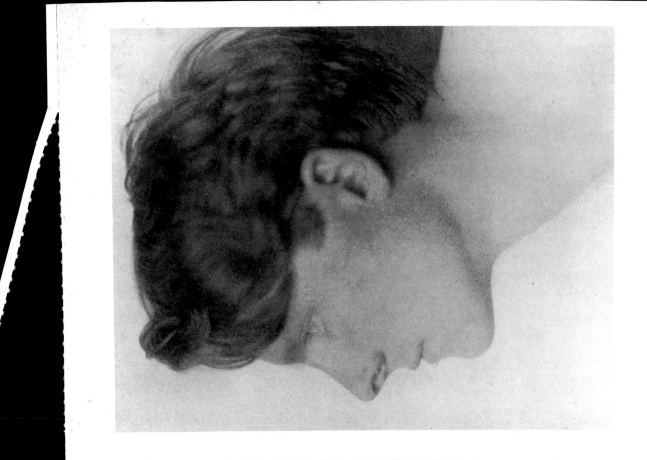

Images of Man

The Poet, Rupert Brooke
By Sherill Schell (American)
Halftone print
from *Photograms of the Year*, 1914–1915

Pomegranate, Box 6099, Rohnert Park, CA 94927

© The Royal Photographic Society

Pomegranate, Box 6099, Rohnert Park, CA 94927

Images of Man

Alphonse Mucha
By Eduard J. Steichen (American, 1879–1973)
Gum platinum print, c. 1900–1901

© The Royal Photographic Society

Pomegranate, Box 6099, Rohnert Park, CA 94927

Images of Man
A. P. Allinson
By Emil Otto Hoppé (German, 1878–1972)
Chlorobromide print, 1909

© The Royal Photographic Society

Pomegranate, Box 6099, Rohnert Park, CA 94927

Images of Man
Augustus John
By Malcolm Arbuthnot (English, 1877–1967)
Platinum print, c. 1911

© The Royal Photographic Society

Pomegranate, Box 6099, Rohnert Park, CA 94927

Images of Man
Negro with Hat, seated
By Fred Holland Day (American, 1864–1933)
Platinum print, c. 1897

© The Royal Photographic Society

Images of Man

Alfred Stieglitz
By Paul Strand (American, 1890–1976)
Bromide print, c. 1924

Pomegranate, Box 6099, Rohnert Park, CA 94927

© The Royal Photographic Society

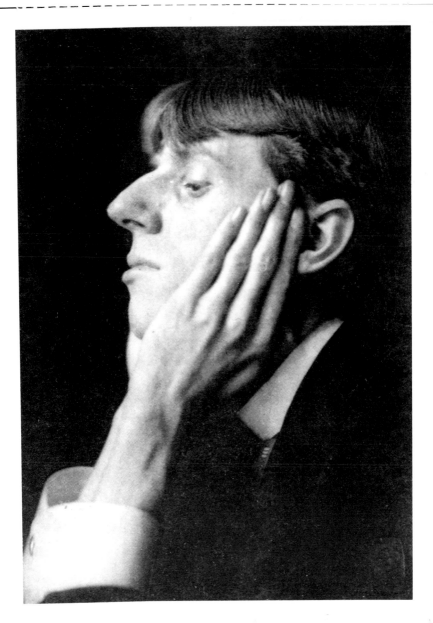

Pomegranate, Box 6099, Rohnert Park, CA 94927

Images of Man
Aubrey Beardsley
By Frederick H. Evans (English, 1853–1943)
Platinum print, c. 1895

© The Royal Photographic Society

Images of Man
W. B. Yeats
By Alvin Langdon Coburn
(English, b. U.S., 1882–1966)
Photogravure, 1908

Pomegranate, Box 6099, Rohnert Park, CA 94927

© The Royal Photographic Society

Pomegranate, Box 6099, Rohnert Park, CA 94927

Images of Man
Samuel L. Clemens (Mark Twain)
By Alvin Langdon Coburn
(English, b. U.S., 1882–1966)
Platinum print, 1905

© The Royal Photographic Society

Images of Man

T. E. Lawrence
By Howard Coster (English, 1885–1959)
Bromide print, 1935

Pomegranate, Box 6099, Rohnert Park, CA 94927

© The Royal Photographic Society

Pomegranate, Box 6099, Rohnert Park, CA 94927

Images of Man
Auguste Rodin
By Alvin Langdon Coburn
(English, b. U. S., 1882–1966)
Photogravure from *Camerawork*, January 1908

© The Royal Photographic Society

Pomegranate, Box 6099, Rohnert Park, CA 94927

Images of Man
Theodore Roosevelt
By Alvin Langdon Coburn
(English, b. U.S., 1882–1966)
Photogravure, c. 1907

© The Royal Photographic Society

Images of Man
Alvin Langdon Coburn
By James Craig Annan (Scottish, 1864–1946)
Carbon print, c. 1906

Pomegranate, Box 6099, Rohnert Park, CA 94927

© The Royal Photographic Society

Images of Man
George Seeley
By Alvin Langdon Coburn
(English, b. U.S., 1882–1966)
Gum platinum print, 1905

Pomegranate, Box 6099, Rohnert Park, CA 94927

© The Royal Photographic Society

Pomegranate, Box 6099, Rohnert Park, CA 94927

Images of Man
Noel Coward
By Dorothy Wilding (English, 1893–1976)
Bromide print, c. 1925

© The Royal Photographic Society

Pomegranate, Box 6099, Rohnert Park, CA 94927

Images of Man

Portrait
By Josef Sudek (Czechoslovakian, 1896–1976)
Chlorobromide print, 1933

© The Royal Photographic Society

Images of Man

Guitar Player of Seville
Baron Adolf De Meyer
(German-American, 1886–1946)
Photogravure from *Camerawork*, October 1908

Pomegranate, Box 6099, Rohnert Park, CA 94927

© The Royal Photographic Society

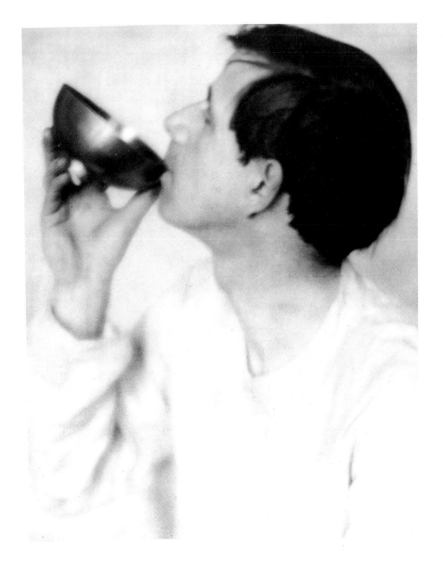

Pomegranate, Box 6099, Rohnert Park, CA 94927

Images of Man
Clarence H. White
By Alvin Langdon Coburn
(English b. U.S., 1882–1966)
Gum platinum print, 1905

© The Royal Photographic Society

Pomegranate, Box 6099, Rohnert Park, CA 94927

Images of Man

Pan

By John Erith

© The Royal Photographic Society